# Delhi, Agra & Jaipur
## *The  Golden  Triangle*

# Delhi, Agra & Jaipur

## The Golden Triangle

## Text
### *Rajaram Panda*

## Published by

## Mittal Publications

*A front view of Red Fort.* **Page no. 2 :** *Qutab Minar behind Alai Darwaza.* **Page no. 4-5 :** *India Gate, a memorial dedicated to the soldiers.*
**Page no. 6-7 :** *A view of Taj Mahal from river side (Agra).* **Page no. 8-9 :** *A front view of Hawa Mahal (Jaipur).*

# DELHI

elhi is, in both the physical and allegorical sense, the gateway of India. It has made captive its very captors, and converted its visitors into residents.

Delhi, the capital city of India, typifies the soul of the country. The city conceals within its bosom annals of civilizations that flourished for more than 3000 years. Indraprastha, according to legends, was founded by the Pandavas in the times of the epic Mahabharata (circa 1500 B.C.), was located near the Old Fort that stands on a large mound overlooking the river Yamuna. The Yamuna has now shifted about two kilometers to the east, but

the Nigambodh Ghat and the Nilichatri temple, believed to have been built by Yudhisthir on its banks, still exist.

There is no general consensus about the origin or evolution of the name Delhi, but it is widely accepted that a city called Dilli was founded by Raja Dhillu- also called Deluthe ruler of Kanauj, in 57 BC. Dilli is believed to have been located between the Qutub area and Tughlaqabad. Ptolemy, the great geographer from Alexandria, who lived between 1 and 2 AD, has recorded the existence of a city called Didala at the site near which Indraprashtha is believed to have been located.

However, modern Delhi is usually said to have come into being when the Tomara Rajputs founded Lal Kot in 736 AD. In 1180, a rival Rajput clan, the Chauhans, ousted the Tomaras and renamed the walled citadel Qila Rai Pithora, the first city of Delhi. Only a few walls of Lal Kot now remain, in the Mehrauli suburb of southwest Delhi, but a stone inscription at the Qutab Minar nearby claims that the stones of the numerous Hindu and Jain temples constructed in Lal Kot were later used to build the Great Mosque in the Qutab complex. Soon afterwards, in the two successive battles of Tarain in 1191, the Rajputs first managed to hold off an invading force from Afghanistan led by Muhammad Ghori, and then succumbed to it a few months later. After establishing his rule in Delhi, Ghori soon returned to Afghanistan, leaving behind his trusted commandant

*Seat of Emperor Shah Jahan, a marble recess of 10 feet high from the ground.*

11

*A wall painting*

*Moti Masjid*

*A wall painting*

*Diwan-I-Am*

and slave Qutb-ud-din Aibak. When Ghori died in 1206, he had no heir, leaving Aibak to declare himself the Sultan of Delhi.

A great devotee of Islam, Aibak destroyed Hindu and Jain temples and built two mosques, one of which still exists in Delhi, the Quwwat-ul-Islam or the Might of Islam, in the Qutab complex. He also began work on the Qutab Minar around 1200 AD to celebrate Islamic dominance in Delhi. For Aibak, the minaret epitomized the eastern extremity of the Islamic faith. An able administrator and a soldier, Aibak, in a short span of four years until his untimely death in 1210, made Delhi his base and annexed a large part of India to the Sultanate.

Qutb-ud-din Aibak was succeeded by Aram Bakhsh, who was soon defeated by Aibak's son-in-law, Illtutmish, the Governor of Badaun and Aibak's former slave. In 1220, Illtutmish completed the Qutab Minar and later extended the Quwwat-ul-Islam mosque. Illtutmish's elder son, groomed to succeed him, died an untimely death. His second son Rukhuddin Firoz took over the throne on his death in 1236, but proved to be incompetent, and was dethroned and killed. Eventually Illtutmish's daughter Raziya Sultana became the first and the only empress to rule Delhi. But her reign was short as the conservatives were against her. In 1290, another group of Turks came to power  the Khiljis. Inspired by Ala-uddin Khilji (1296-1316), they extended their dominion to the deccan plateau of central India.

His reign, the pinnacle of the Delhi Sultanate, was marked by agrarian reforms, and the establishment in 1303 of Siri, the second city of Delhi, built in characteristically ornate marble and red sandstone. Near present-day Hauz Khas, it grew into a flourishing commercial center. Ala-uddin died a disappointed man.

In 1320 Ghiyasuddin Tughlaq proclaimed himself Sultan. He built a city fortress, at Tughlaqabad, 8km east of Qutab, but Delhi's third city was occupied for just five years from 1321, when the capital was shifted 1100 km south to Daulatabad in Maharashtra at great human cost. Apart from the ramparts encompassing the crumbling ruins, and the odd building and tomb, little now remains of this third settlement. Water scarcity drove the Tughlaqs back to Delhi in 1327, and as a recompense for the mistake, a new city, Jahanpanah, was built between Lal Kot and Siri by the eccentric Muhammad bin Tughlaq to protect the vulnerable open plain. The energies of the next sultan, Feroz Shah, were taken up with suppressing rebellion, as the sultanate began to disintegrate, but his reputation as an iconoclast is belied by his keen interest in Indian culture and history. Fascinated by the Ashokan pillars of Meerut and Topra, he had them moved to the new capital, the fifth city of Delhi, Firozabad, built beside the river Yamuna in 1354. On a fertile piece of land extending from Hauz Khas to Kotla Ferozshah. This beautiful city had lovely gardens, forts, mosques and towns, which were later ravaged by Sher Shah Suri.

The Tughlaq dynasty came to an end in 1398, when Timur (Tamerlane), a Central Asian Turk, sacked Delhi. His successors, the Sayyids (1414-44), were ousted by Buhlul Lodi who established a dynasty that left behind the fine tombs and mosques still to be seen in the beautiful Lodi Gardens. As the Lodi sultans became more absolute, they made many enemies among the nobles, especially the governors of Punjab and Sind, who invited Babur (a descendant of Genghis Khan) and Timur, who was seeking his fortune in Afghanistan, to come to their aid. The Lodi dynasty ended when Sultan Ibrahim Lodi died in battle, fighting the brilliant and enigmatic Babur on the plain of Panipat just north of Delhi in 1526. Babur's victory marked the dawn of the Moghul (a derivative of Mongol) dynasty, whose lengthy sojourn in power led to the eventual realization of the dream of an Indian empire that had so eluded the earlier Delhi Sultans.

*Red Fort*

*A wall painting*

*Wall behind Emperor Seat*

*A wall painting*

13

*Different views of Akshardham Temple*

*A general view of Qutab Minar*

Agra remained Babur's capital during his brief rule of four years, but his eldest son Humayun chose to govern from Delhi after his father's death in 1530. He built a new city at the old fort named Dinapanah, also the location of the Pandavas of the Mahabharata. Humayun's reign of a decade was cut short when Sher Shah Suri, a trusted general of Ibrahim Lodhi defeated him. Proving to be a very efficient ruler, Sher Shah Suri strengthened and extended both his empire and the Dinpanath city and renamed it Shergarh. These constituted the sixth ancient city of Delhi. After a 15-year exile, Humayun was able to recapture his throne from Sher Shah Suri's nephew. But, destiny willed otherwise. Humayun had ruled only for about a year during his second phase when he met with an accident and died.

*A view from the first storey of Qutab Minar*

15

*Iron Pillar situated in the centre of courtyard of the mosque Quwwat-ul-Islam*
**Page no. 16** : *Close view of Qutab Minar*

In 1556, his 13-year-old son Akbar became the third Mughal monarch of India. A contemporary of Queen Elizabeth I, he is considered the most distinguished of all the kings of his dynasty. His endearing qualities included a tolerant attitude towards Hinduism and other religions, and, benevolence towards all. During his long and efficient rule of half a century, Delhi remained his capital for only eight years, as he decided to govern from Agra and Fetehpur Sikri.

Delhi remained a provincial city for both him and his son Jahangir. It was his grandson Shah Jahan who was ultimately responsible for restoring the imperial glory of Delhi. Akbar's grandson, in 1628, who assumed the title Shah Jahan, "Ruler of the Universe", and began a fruitful and

*Qutab Minar*

*Qutab Minar*

*Tomb of Altamish*

*Qutab Minar*

extravagant reign that oversaw the construction of some of the finest Moghul monuments, including the Taj Mahal in Agra. The new walled capital of Shahjahanabad, the seventh city, which is now Old Delhi, incorporated the Red Fort as its citadel had the River Yamuna as its backdrop. It covered an area from present day Kashmiri Gate to Delhi Gate and had 14 imposing doorways, out of which, only five have survived. The majestic city had beautiful palaces, forts, mosques, gardens, houses and bazaars. Jama Masjid, the largest mosque in India, was also constructed by him as also Chandni Chowk or the silver street which was the heart of the city and a historic thoroughfare. Shah Jahan was deposed (and imprisoned in Agra) by his ruthless son, Aurangzeb, who ruled from Delhi until 1681, when he transferred the capital to the Deccan plateau until his death in 1707.

For the next sixty years, Delhi's government was controlled by courtiers, and the city fell victim to successive invasions. In 1739, Nadir Shah, the emperor of Persia, swept across north India and overcame Muhammad Shah in the Red Fort, taking away precious booty and wiping out much of the local population. The relatively plain tomb of Safdarjung (near the Lodi Gardens), built in 1754 for Emperor Mirza Khan in the same style as the Taj, yet lacking the marble and rich decoration, demonstrates the decline of Moghul power. Soon after, in 1760, the Hindu Marathas and Jats, in the wake of fading Moghul supremacy, combined forces against the rulers and besieged and looted the Red Fort, but did not take power.

The Moghul rulers were reduced to puppet kings, and the British, who had already gained footholds in Madras and Bengal under the guise of the East India Company, moved to Delhi in 1803 during the

*Lotus Temple, an architectural marvel of the Bahai faith.*

reign of the Moghul emperor, Bahadur Shah. They swiftly took control, leaving Bahadur Shah with his palace and his pension, but no power.

The accession of Edward VII to the throne of England in 1903 was celebrated at a grand durbar followed by another one in 1911, where George V announced the shifting of the British Indian capital to Delhi from Calcutta. Two famous British architects, Sir Edwin Lutyens and Sir Herbert Baker, were assigned the project of building the new capital. Raisina Hill was chosen as the pivotal point for the Viceroy Lodge, now known as Rashtrapati Bhavan, around which the other important administrative centers had to be built. New Delhi was declared as the formal capital of the British India Empire in January 1931 and this was the eighth city of Delhi. Its fortunes again soared when New Delhi was retained as the capital of independent India.

*Chhattarpur Temple*

A procession on the Republic Day at Rajpath

**Page no. 20 :** India Gate, a 42 m memorial, features an eternal flame.

**Page no. 21 Top :** Rashtrapati Bhawan

**Below :** Mughal Garden inside Rashtrapati Bhawan

Delhi's precious monumental heritage is also interlinked with its distinguished history; the study of one giving an insight into the other. The 1,300 listed monuments of Delhi's ancient and modern cities now in varying degrees of preservation, reflect each phase of Indo-Islamic architecture. All that remains of the city of Lalkot and Qila Rai Pithora are ruins of the first defensive wall and some broken structures in Surajkund and Aanagpur dam. The 4th century Iron Pillar (a metallurgical wonder with Sanskrit inscriptions) that has remained rust and corrosion free till today, was brought by Anang Pal and installed in a Vishnu Temple which later became the site of Quwwat-ul-Islam mosque built by Qutbuddin Aibek. He mercilessly pulled down all Hindu and Jain temples and used the material for his construction work. This mosque was the first in northern India and had a lot of Hindu

*India Gate in the night*

*Parliament House*

*Page no. 23 :*
***Top :***
*Central Secretariat
in the night*

***Below :***
*Central Secretariat
in the morning*

ornamentations like tasseled ropes, bells, flowers and sculptures on its pillars and corridors. Nearby, he raised the towering minaret, the Qutub Minar, one of Delhi's landmarks. It was built to celebrate Ghori's victory over the Rajputs. The Minar is a five-storey building with a height of 72.5 metres. The first storey of the Qutub Minar was completed in the lifetime of Qutbuddin. His son-in-law and successor, Illtatmish, added the next three storeys. Other architectural gems within this complex include the tomb of Illtatmish, built by himself in 1235 A.D., is a beautiful example of the fusion of Hindu art with Islamic design. And the Alai Darwaza, in red sandstone and marble was built by Allauddin Khilji in 1311 as a southern gateway to the mosque.

*Dandi March*

24

*Safdarjung Tomb*

Delhi's fourth city, Jahanpanah has practically disappeared but its fifth, Firoz Shah Kotla rises off Bahadur Shah Zafar Marg and is well known for its Ashokan pillar which the Sultan brought from Mathura & Topra. Timur devastated Delhi in 1398 and as a result the 15th century saw little growth. So, the few monuments they built are simple and devoid of intricate ornamentation and other embellishments. The tomb of Mohammed Shah Sayyid in the Lodi Gardens, one of the Delhi's most beautiful gardens, is a large octagonal structure with massive arcades, pavilions and a large central dome. The Bada Gumbad has a mosque decorated not with carvings but inscriptions and foliage designs in plaster. The blue-glazed tiles in the interior of Sheesh Gumbad give it a glass-like appearance. The Lodis too did not use red sandstone or expensive marble and their grey granite tombs were small but sturdy and set the trend for the early garden tomb. The tomb of Sikandar Lodi arouses interest because of its unusual styled dome in different coloured tiles.

Around 1311, Allaudin Khilji established Siri, the second city and dug a vast reservoir with its stone steps at Hauz Khas. Very little remains of Siri is left, but Hauz Khas was extensively renovated a few decades later. Now, ethnic boutiques and cafes dot the Hauz Khas village and the location is as attractive as the exclusive goods on sale. The great fort of Tughlaqabad built between 1320-1324 by Ghiyasuddin as a protection against Mongol raids became Delhi's third city. The fort and tomb are characteristic of robust Tughlaq architecture. The fort was never attacked but was plundered for its building material by Mohammed Tughlaq.

*Lodhi Garden*

*Gurudwara (Bangla Sahib)*
***Below :** A Sikh procession outside Gurudwara*

In 1526, Babur founded the Mughal empire in India. The impressive Purana Qila, Delhi's sixth city, is a combined effort of his son Humayun and the Afghan Sher Shah Suri who temporarily deposed him. Purana Qila is a monument of bold design which is strong, straight forward and every inch a fortress. The Purana Qila has three gates Humayun Darwaza, Talaqi Darwaza and Bara Darwaza. The present entrance is the Bara Darwaza, an imposing red sandstone gate on the western wall. The fort contains a fine mosque Quilla-e-Kunha founded by Sher Shah in Indo-Afghan sculpture and the Sher Mandal, a two-storied octagonal pavilion in red sandstone, built by Sher Shah. Humayun used it as a library after he captured the fort. However, the Mandal is tragic, since it was here where the emperor is said to have tripped on its tortuous stairs and tumbled to his death in 1556. Humayun's Tomb situated to the south of old fort and near the holy pilgrim center Nizamuddin Auliya is a fabulous structure built by his wife Haji Begum in 1556. The colossal red-sandtone tomb with an octagonal shape faces a Charbagh. It was designed by a Persian

26

*Indira Gandhi Memorial*

architect named Mirak Mirza Ghujas, and completed in 1565, the edifice was a trendsetter of the time. It is said that all later Mughal monuments, including the Taj Mahal, followed its design. Nearby are the Zoo, the Crafts Museum, where craftsmen work in a simulated rural setting, and Pragati Maidan, the exhibition grounds.

In April 1639 the Mughal emperor Shah Jahan laid the foundation of Shahjahanabad, Delhi's seventh city, and it epitomized the grandeur of his empire. His seat of power was the impressive Lal Qila or the Red Fort. Chiselled out of red sandstone, the entire complex comprised Moti Mahal, Rang Mahal, Sheesh Mahal and Khas Mahal, Diwan-I-am and Diwan-I-Khas with rows of beautiful cusped arches in marble, the Pearl Mosque, the hammams or lavish bathrooms, and exquisitely laid-out gardens. The Pietra Dura work on the recess behind the balcony was executed by a French artificer Austin De-Bordeux. The famous "Peacock throne" also stood in Diwan-I-Khas, which was taken by

Nadir Shah, is at present in Persia. The fort has two main entrances Delhi Gate and Lahore Gate. The later get its name from the fact that it faces Lahore in Pakistan. It's entrance leads to Delhi's most crowded bazaar, Chandni Chowk. This was once a tree-lined bazaar with a canal flowing through its center. Today, it is one of the largest trading centers in northern India-thriving, congested and chaotic. Each of its bylanes leads into a world of spices or silver or perfumes or textiles. Chandni Chowk is also replete with historical landmarks. One of them being Jain Temple built in 1656 A.D. Located next to it is the Gauri Shankar Temple. The imposing Town Hall built in 1866 A.D. today houses the offices of the Delhi Municipal Corporation, and is the center of Civic Administration of New Delhi. And on the western end of Chandni Chowk is the Fatehpuri Mosque. It is built of red sandstone paved with black and white marble tiles. The mosque was constructed in 1650 A.D. by Begum Fatehpuri, one of the wives of Emperor Shahjahan. There is a spacious courtyard and a fountain in its center. Opposite the

*National Museum*

**Top:** *Humayun's mausoleum is the first mughal garden tomb.* **Bottom (L):** *Intricate Jaali work on windows inside Humayun's Tomb* **Bottom (Right Above):** *The emperor's cenotaph* **Bottom (Right Below):** *Subsidiary tomb chamber to the north-west of the main tomb chamber*

*Raj Ghat (Mahatma Gandhi Samadhi)*
*Page no. 28 : Humayun's Tomb*

Red Fort is the Jama Masjid, India's largest mosque. It is built of red sandstone with decoration in white marble. Each minar possessing 130 steps. From the top of the minars, an enchanting Bird eye view of the city is available.

New Delhi was built in 1911. Lutyens and Baker planned a city with wide, tree-lined avenues. The 340-roomed Viceroy Lodge, now the Rashtrapati Bhawan, was raised on Raisina Hill. The most magnificent room in the Rashtrapati Bhavan is the Durbar Hall, which lies directly beneath the main dome. All important Indian State and Official ceremonies are held here. To the west, is the famous and beautifully landscaped Mughal Gardens, designed after the terraced gardens the Mughals built in Kashmir. The gardens is famous as the 'Butterfly Garden' for the numerous butterflies that visit the varied flowers. The garden is open to the public in February. Nearby are Secretariat buildings comprising the North and South Block stand facing each other on either side of Rajpath. India Gate a memorial to the 90,000 Indian soldiers who died in World War I, circular-shaped colonnaded

30

*Jantar Mantar observatory*

Parliament House, the prestigious National Museum, the National Gallery of Modern Art, On Republic day, Rajpath witnesses a display of pageantry.

The classy commercial center of Connaught Place was planned as part of New Delhi. Alongwith stalls on Janpath, and emporia on Baba Kharak Singh Marg, it is a shopper's paradise. Rather characteristically, an 18th century masonry observatory, the Jantar Mantar, built by Raja Jai singh II of Jaipur, lies in the midst of this commercial area.

Other major attractions are Lotus Temple, a temple that delicately unfurls like a lotus in bloom, Raj Ghat and other memorials, the colourful Birla Temple, the Buddha Jayanti and Nehru Park, Delhi Haat, which informally presents an all fresco bazaar of crafts and cuisine from all over the country.

*Inside Jantar Mantar observatory*

*Red Fort as viewed from Chandni Chowk*

*Delli Haat*

*Celebrations of the Dussera Festival at parade ground opposite Red Fort*

**Page no. 32 : Top :** *Old Fort*
**Below :** *Old Delhi Railway Station in the night*

Delhi's population of more than fifteen million belongs to people of all castes and religions, so there is an interesting diversity of style and culture which extends to its climate also.

33

*Jama Masjid is the largest and the grandest mosque in India. It can accommodate more than 20,000 worshipers at a time during festivals*

*Lord Ganesh*
***Page no. 35 :***
*A front view of Birla Temple*

*Lord Shiva*
*Centre : Laxmi Narayan*

*Lord Vishnu*

Delhi is pulsating with music concerts, dance festivals, theatre performances and art exhibitions.

Delhi is a true cosmopolitan city ever on the move, always open to change encouraging, absorbing and assimilating new ideas in every sphere.

*Lord Hanuman*

*Lord Krishna*
*Centre : Lord Buddha*

*Goddess Durga*

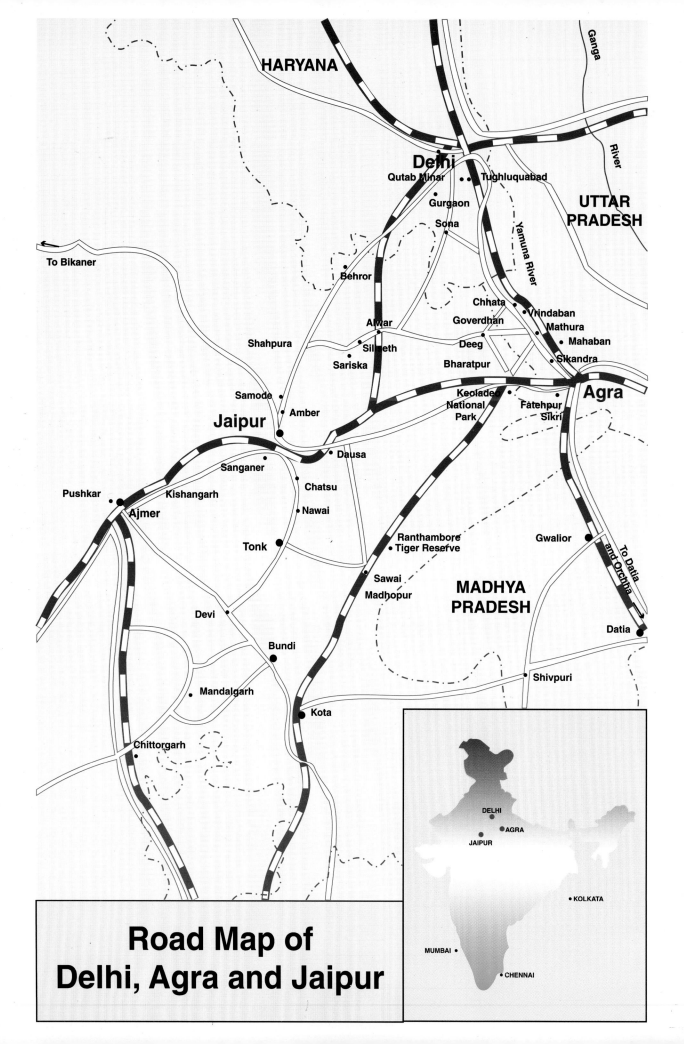

# Road Map of
# Delhi, Agra and Jaipur

# AGRA

*A front view of Taj Mahal*
**Page no. 37 :** *A view of Taj Mahal*

On the Western bank of the River Yamuna, Agra is just over 200 km from Delhi. The Hindu epic Mahabharata refers to it as 'Agraban', part of Brij Bhoomi, the homeland of Lord Krishna. The earliest recorded history of Agra, however, is its establishment by a local king Raja Badal Singh in 1475. It grew into an important power center under the Delhi Sultan Sikandar Lodi, who shifted his capital from Delhi in 1504.

Agra grew into an important cultural and commercial center in 1500 AD. After Sikandar's death, his son Ibrahim Lodi lost the first Battle of Panipat in 1526 AD to Babur, an Afghan noble, who became the first Mughal monarch. The Mughal Emperor Babur took upon himself the task for rendering Agra, a unique character and beauty of its own. Emperor Babur brought a change in the culture and lifestyle among the people of Agra, which then brought forth some of the finest craftsmen, artists, statesmen, warriors and nobility, this part of India had ever witnessed. The

*Taj Mahal*
**Page no. 40-41 :** *A view of Taj Mahal from the garden*

golden age of Agra's history, thus began to set in. Babur, in his brief but eventful reign, built **Rambagh** in 1528, the first Persian Charbagh with symmetrical pathways, fountains and running water. It is believed that he was buried before being permanently interred at Kabul in Afghanistan.

His son Humayun, built a new capital city-Dinapanah-in Delhi but his grandson Akbar, the greatest Mughal ruler, returned to Agra, to build himself the strong and robust Agra Fort. It was designed and built by Akbar in 1565 A.D. The fort was ready by 1571 though additions were made up until the rule of Shahjahan. During the time of Akbar the fort mainly served military purpose, while by the time of Shahjahan it also served as a palace and court.

The fort has four gates and is enclosed by a double barricaded 70 ft. high wall of red sand stone. Many buildings were constructed within the fort of which very few remain till date. One of the most significant ones is the multi

*The main entrance of Taj Mahal*

*Taj Mahal*

storied Jahangir Mahal built by Akbar for his wife Jodha Bai. The Mahal is reached through an impressive Amar Singh Gate built by Akbar and its inner courtyard consists of beautiful halls, profuse carvings on stone, exquisitely carved heavy brackets, piers and cross beams. Jahangir Mahal mixes Transoxanian (Central Asian) features with courtyard halls styled in the broader Gujarat-Malwa-Rajasthan tradition as it had been passed onto the Mughals by the early 16th century architecture of Raja Man Singh of Gwalior.

The **Khas Mahal**, built by Shahjahan, is an airy edifice overlooking the specially laid Angoori Bagh (Grape garden - a simple formal Mughal garden). **Sheesh Mahal** (Mirror Palace) or the royal hamman (bath) is decorated with myriad glass pieces and a central fountain. **Musamman Burj** (a octagonal tower) within the Agra fort is the most romantic, ornamental pavilion wherein lived two most beautiful and powerful Mughal queens -

*Details of Taj Mahal*

*Taj Mahal*

Nurjahan (Jahangirs's chief Queen) and Mumtaz Mahal (Shahjahan's chief Queen). The quality of pietra dura (stone inlay work) decoration is fabulous and perfect. Here Shahjahan spent his last few years as a captive held by Aurangzeb (Shahjahan's son). Shahjahan languished and died looking at the Taj Mahal.

**Diwan-I-Khas** (Hall of Private audience) was built by Shahjahan in 1636-37 and is a small hall with double marble columns inlaid with peitra dura decoration. Here the Mughal Emperor received important dignitaries or foreign ambassadors. Below lies the grand courtyard of **Machchi Bhawan**, meant for harem functions had fountains, tanks and water channels stocked with fish. On another side stands a small mosque **Nagina Masjid**

built in marble by Shahjahan to be used exclusively by the women of the zenana or harem. **Diwan-I-Aam** (hall of Public Audience) was built by Shahjahan who repalaced an earlier wooden structure. Here the emperor met officials and listened to petitioners. The famous Peacock Throne ordered by Shahjahan was also kept here. Further north

*Details of Taj Mahal*

44

*Taj Mahal*

*Page no. 45 :*
*The cenotaphs of*
*Emperor Shah Jahan*
*and his wife*
*Mumtaz Mahal*

*Page no. 46-47 :*
*An evening view*
*of*
*Taj Mahal*
*from back side*

stands the **Moti Masjid** (Pearl Mosque), its three domes in white marble raising their heads over the red sandstone wall. Moti Masjid is known for its sheer grandeur and perfect proportions. Nearby was the Ladies **Meena Bazaar**, where female merchants came to sell goods to the ladies of the Mughal Court. No males were allowed to enter the bazaar except Akbar, though according to one apocryphal story he still enjoyed visiting in female disguise. It is still remembered as the place where Shahjahan first met the beautiful Arjumand Bana (Later Mumtaz Mahal).

Akbar had established himself as a great and powerful monarch with his empire expanding steadily over the years. He decided to build a magnificent

*Details of Taj Mahal*

*Darshani Gate, the third entrance of Agra Fort*
**Page no. 49 :** *Different views and effects of Taj Mahal*
**Page no. 50 :** *Details of the interior of Taj Mahal*

enclosed space surrounded by colonnades and has a large open area where petitioners and courtiers once stood in attendance; Diwan-I-Khas (hall of Private Audience) - used for serious, confidential, diplomatic and religious discourses - is famous for its central decorated pillar consisting of 36 elegantly carved brackets in the Gujarati style-heavy and ornate, and sprouting in shape; Panch Mahal (five-tiered palace) is an intriguing five-storied pavilion of winds. It was Akbar's personal citadel for pleasure and relaxation. Each storey is pillared and is smaller than the others as one ascends. The buildings resemble a Buddhist temple. It tapers from the ground floor with 84 columns to its domed top supported by only four columns. The Turkish Sultan's palace is known for exquisitely carved panels

city, Fatehpur Sikri the city of victory, on a rocky ridge, 37 kms from the city of Agra. It was built by the Mughal Emperor Akbar between 1571 and 1584. The buildings within Fatehpur Sikri are a unique blend of different architectural traditions. Though the general layout and concept of the buildings conform to the Islamic style of architecture, the actual buildings (mainly palaces), their ornate columns, arches, carving style, etc., show a strong Hindu style in general and that of Gujarat and Rajasthan in particular.

There are a number of buildings within the Fatehpur Sikri complex. Diwan-I-Aam (hall of Public Audience) is an

*Statue of Shivaji Smarak, outside Agra Fort*
**Page no. 51 :** *Different views and details of Taj Mahal*
**Page no. 52 :** *Different views and special effects of Taj Mahal*

*Jahangir Mahal*
***Page no. 54 -55 :*** *Amar Singh Gate, the main entrance of Agra Fort*

depicting wildlife-lions, birds, and foliage. Anup Talab where the famous court musician Tansen played music.

Jodha Bai's palace (Jodha Bai was Akbar's Rajput queen) has the most distinctively Gujarati and Rajasthani architectural features. Also noteworthy are mariam's Palace or Sunehra Makan (golden house), Palace of Birbal (one of Akbar's minister notable for his witticisms) and a miniature garden. Jami Masjid (mosque), sacred center of Sikri, symbolizes the city's spiritual prominence. In the vast courtyard stands the tomb of Sheikh Salim Chisti who is said to have granted Akbar and his Hindu queen Jodhabai their wish for a son. His blessings are still sought by childless women. The tombstone of

the saint lies under a beautiful canopy made of ebony, brass, mother of pearl and lapis lazuli. The main entrance to Fatehpur Sikri is through the 175 feet Buland Darwaza, the highest southern gateway in the world. It was built by Akbar to commemorate his victory over Khandesh in Gujarat.

*Diwan-I-Aam*

56

*Water Gate*

Akbar's passion for building made him plan his own mausoleum for which he selected a site, eight kms on the outskirts of Agra named Sikandarabad, after Sikandar Lodi. But, after Akbar's death, his son Jahangir completed the tomb in 1613.

This richly decorated structure is a quaint mixture of styles. A magnificent marble-inlaid gateway leads up to the open, airy, four-tiered structure which is topped by a white marble cenotaph and screen on the fifth storey. The main entrance is through an imposing southern gateway of red sandstone with decorative inlay work in black, white and yellow marble, creating beautiful floral and geometric patterns and fine calligraphy of Koranic verses. The garden tomb at the center of the Persian Charbagh can be reached from the gateways leading to wide pathways which divide the area into four quadrants. The main tomb is a bright red, five-tiered pyramidal structure

*Golden Pavilion*

*Suman Burj*

quite reminiscent of Akbar's buildings in Fatehpur Sikri.

The first floor is a podium of arches with a doorway decorated with inlay work. The next three storeys have earthy sandstone pavilions with a flat roof and no arches topped by an open terrace intricately designed with latticed marble screens. Each screen has arches with a panel inscribed with Persian couplets. In the center lies the replica tomb of Akbar, carved out of a single block of white marble, embellished with floral motifs and inscriptions carrying the 99 names of Allah. It is said that initially the roof was covered with a canopy made of gold, silver, brocade and precious stones and the famous Kohinoor Diamond, which is now in British possession. The real cenotaph,

*Marble Fountain inside Suman Burj*

*Khas Mahal*

is in unostentatious and plain sandstone and lies protected inside a dimly-lit chamber which can be reached down through a sloping passage. The mausoleum represents Akbar's philosophy and secular outlook blending Islamic, Hindu, Buddhist, Jain and Christian motifs and styles.

Akbar's son Jahangir continued to rule from Agra but his love for a life of pleasure made him spend most of his time in the idyllic Kashmir Valley and his wife Nur Jahan managed the state affairs. He beautified Agra with palaces and gardens.

To the north of the fort, on the opposite bank of the Yamuna lies **Itmad-ud-daulah**, the tomb of Mirza Ghiyas Beg, Jahangir's wazir. Also known as the 'baby Taj', it was the first Mughal

*Diwan-I-Khas*

*Amar Singh Gate in the Night*

*Diwan-I-Aam*

*Interior of Diwan-I-Aam*

*Suman Burj*

structure totally built from marble and first to make extensive use of pietra dura stone inlay with semi-precious stones like lapis lazuli, agate, jasper and onyx. The tomb was built by Empress Noor Jahan, in memory of her father, Ghias-ud-Din Beg in 1622-25 A.D. This ornate tomb is considered a precursor of the Taj Mahal. This small garden tomb reflects the taste and sophistication of the gifted queen. The warm yellow marble is highlighted with white and black marble inlay, and the lacey pierced marble screens and rich, jewel-inlaid mosaics have a delicate, feminine quality that is pure enchantment.

After Emperor Jahangir's death, Prince Khurram managed to claim the throne after a lot of bloodshed and became Shah Jahan or the conqueror of the world in 1628. Shahjahan ascended to the throne of Mughal Empire. He marked the zenith of Mughal architecture, when he built the Taj in memory of his beloved wife Mumtaz Mahal.

Mumtaz Mahal the second, wife of Shah Jahan was accompanying him on one of his military expedition where she developed complications and died while delivering her 14th child. A devastated Shah Jahan had only one mission left in life, to fulfil his wife's last desire by constructing a monument peerless in both concept and beauty, and which would symbolize their eternal love for each other.

It is estimated that nearly 20,000 workers consisting of labourers, carpenters, craftsman, artists and engineers worked incessantly for almost 22 years (1631-1653). The Taj Mahal is a total package of tomb, mosque, gardens, gateways and fountains.

*Itmad-Ud-Daula's Tomb*

Taj Mahal is placed on a high plinth (platform), 6.7 m (21.98 ft) high and covers an area of 95 sq m (1,022.57 square feet). There are four elegant tapering minarets, one on each corner of the plinth. Each of the minarets is 41.6 m (136.48 ft) high and is capped by a small cupola. The minarets, not only balance the main structure of the mausoleum, but are also placed in such a way that in case of a mishap, they do not fall over the main edifice. Each pillar has a letter written on it, which put together spell the word ar-rahman (all merciful) - one of the many names of Allah.

The main structure of the Taj Mahal is square and is beveled at its corners.

*Details of Itmad-Ud-Daula's Tomb*

61

*Interior of Itmad-Ud-Daula's Tomb*

Each side of the Taj Mahal is 56.6 m (185.69 ft) long. On each faôade, arched recesses arranged in two stories flank a high diwan in the center. The top border of the diwan on each side rises higher than the rest of faôade, thus concealing the neck of the dome behind it. The outer walls of the Taj Mahal are decorated in a number of places with shallow marble carving apart from the elegant pieta dura work, which can be seen near arched recesses and borders. The entrance to the tomb leads you to the central hall, which houses the false tombs and has four small octagonal halls, grouped around it. The original graves are located in crypt, which is directly below the central hall. The cenotaphs are decorated with exquisite

*Dayal Bagh*

62

*The main entrance of Akbar Tomb*

pietra dura (stone inlay) work. Apart from unexcelled inlay work the cenotaph of Mumtaz Mahal is inscribed by 99 different names of Allah. It is said that as many as 35 different types of precious and semi-precious stones were used in the inlay work done on the Taj. The white marble came from Makrana in Rajasthan and the red sandstone from Fatehpur Sikri. Precious stories like jade, crystal, turquoise, lapis lazuli, sapphire, coral and diamonds were brought from far-flung places in Tibet, China, Sri Lanka, Persia and Afghanistan. It is believed that a fleet of 1000 elephants was used to transport the material.

Declared a world Heritage Site by the UNESCO, the Taj Mahal has always evoked varying emotions from wonder to ecstasy and often times, inspired

*Akbar Tomb*

*Bulland Gate, Fatehpur Sikri*
***Page no. 64-65 :*** *The Tomb of Sheikh Salim Chistie*

poetic verse. Over the centuries, it has become the symbol of undying love and flawless beauty. Environmentalists are concerned about the possible hazardous effects of pollution on this marble wonder and are taking steps to preserve it for posterity.

Shahjahan's son Auranzeb was unpopular with his people because of his authoritarian ways. The Mughal empire slowly began to disintegrate and by 1711, Agra was an undefended hunting ground for the Jats, Rohillas, Marathas and finally, the British. In 1935, Agra was combined with Oudh to form the United Provinces which was renamed Uttar Pradesh after India became independent in 1947.

Besides being a historic city, Agra has shades of modernity as is typical of any Indian city. Agra is also a popular destination amongst shoppers. The most important being marble and wood items inlaid with colored stones, similar to the pietra dura work on Taj Mahal. This apart, Agra is also famous for other variety of handicrafts including leather goods, jewellery, dhurrie (rug) weaving, brassware, carpets and embroidery work. Agra is also home to one of the finest exhibits of village crafts in the form of Shilpgram - a crafts village and open-air emporium with a wide range of crafts from all over the country. The Taj Ganj area that had sprung up near Taj Mahal has a number of makeshift eateries catering to budget travelers.

*A general view of Fatehpur Sikri*

Agra is also famous for some of its local sweets like petha and gazak, and saltish snack called dalmoth.

The narrow lanes of Agra filled with the aroma of Mughlai Cuisine, the craftsman who are busy in creating master pieces with their skill, all remind of the Mughal royalty which this city had once experienced.

Agra therefore holds its place in the annals of history as the heart of social political, economic, and artistic life of India. The present day city of Agra has lived up to this image and a visit to this part of the world will ensure, among other things, the memories of the Taj Mahal.

*Hiran Minar*
***Page no. 68 :*** *Different views and palaces of Fatehpur sikri*

# JAIPUR
## The Pink City

*Hawa Mahal (Palace of winds)*

Jaipur the capital city of the northern Indian state of Rajasthan is one of the most vibrant and colourful cities of India. Famous for its colourful culture, forts, palaces, and lakes, the city basks in the glory of a rich and eventful past.

Jaipur gets its name from its founder Maharaja Jai Singh II, the great warrior and astronomer, who ruled between 1693 and 1743. Jai Singh's lineage can be traced back to the Kucchwaha Rajput clan who came to power in the 12th century.

Duleh Rai was a Kachhawahas who could trace his lineage to Rama, hero of the sun-born dynasty immortalized in Ramayana. He was married to the daughter of Chauhans of Ajmer. Duleh Rai's also known as 'Tej Karan', his son Kakil Dev is known to have established dynastic rule in Amber which was the most important stronghold of the Minas.

The Kachhawahas, despite being devout Hindu belonging to the Kshtriya (warrior) caste, recognized the expediency of aligning themselves with

*Jaipur Museum, situated in the Ram Niwas Garden*
**Page no. 70 :** *Tourists enjoying the elephant ride while ascending the Amer Fort.*
**Page no. 71 :** *Hawa Mahal*

the powerful Mughal Empire. They paid homage at the Mughal court, and cemented the relationship with marital alliances. They were handsomely rewarded for their bravery defending the Mughals in their various skirmishes. With war loots they were able to finance construction of the fortress palace at **Amber**, which began in 1592 by **Maharaja Man Singh** (1590-1619) the Rajput commander of Akbar's Army. He had a multi-faceted personality with varied interests. He started ateliers and departments devoted to art, crafts, literature and the performing arts.

**Amber** was the capital of Kachhawa Rajput Kings. Amer is a city of natural hill fortifications, and red sand stone palaces. The entrance to the historic

Amber Fort is through the arched gateway of Surajpol leading into the Jaleb Chowk or the grand square courtyard, now inhabited with shops. A few steps to the right lead to the beautifully-carved silver doors of the sacred Shila Devi Temple which enshrines the war-goddess Kali, the family deity of the Kachchwaha clan. The image in the form of a stone was brought by Raja Man Singh I from Bengal. The second courtyard takes us to the spectacular Diwan-I-Am built by Jai Singh I. This open pavilion with double row of marble and red sandstone pillars with finely-carved elephant brackets, frescoes and latticed galleries speak of a strong Mughal influence. To the right is Ganesh Pol, a massive two-storeyed ceremonial gateway, exuberantly embellished with floral

72

*City Gate is one of the many gates of Jaipur*

motifs, glass mosaics, frescoes, latticed-stone galleries and a painting of Lord Ganesh, the god of learning and good fortune, which leads to the third court. Here, three private palace apartments are built around Aram Bagh, an ornamental Mughal garden. To the right is Sukh Niwas or the hall of pleasure with ivory-inlaid fragrant sandalwood doors. Its elaborate fountains and black and white marble chutes keep the interiors cool and refreshing. At the other end of the garden is Jai Mandir, the private apartments of Jai Singh I, said to be the most exquisitely decorated of all Rajasthani palaces. The Jai Mahal, on the ground floor, has scalloped arches decorated with flowers and butterflies and the exotic Sheesh Mahal is embedded with mirrors that twinkle like a starlit sky when a candle flame is lit inside its closed doors.

The Jas Mandir close by, is famous for its glass inlay, alabaster relief work on its ceiling, latticed windows and very fine marble screens which bring in fresh breeze and also provide a panoramic view of Dilaram Bagh set amidst the Maota Lake. Narrow passages from the garden court lead to the fourth court surrounded by Raja Man Singh's palace and the zenana or the apartments for his 12 queens.

The Chand Pol, right opposite the Suraj Pol leads to a pathway overlooking the Kadmi Palace, the earlier citadel of the Kachchwahas. Amer is also well known for temples that are still in use, like the 15th century Narsimha temple, the famous

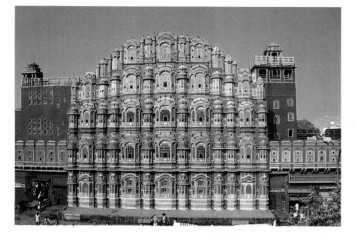

76

*Ram bagh Palace*
**Below :** *Gaitor*

**Page no. 74-75 :**
*An overview of
Hawa Mahal
from 'main bazaar'*

**Page no. 76 :**
*Different views and
effects of Hawa Mahal*

Jagat Siromani temple built by Man Singh in the memory of his son and a Shiva temple of Ambikeshwara, from which the city is said to have derived its name.

Sawai Jai Singh II became an influential administrative and diplomatic adviser during Aurangzeb's rule and this led to a dramatic increase in the strength and stature of Amber. The wealth of the kingdom increased exponentially, and this together with the need to accommodate the ever burgeoning population and a paucity of water at the old capital Amber, prompted the Maharaja in 1727 to commence work on a new city he named after himself - Jaipur. The foundation stone of this well-planned beautiful city which was to be constructed from start to finish was laid on November 25, 1727 below the protective environs of the Nahargarh fort towards the south of Amber.

Much of the credit for Jaipur goes to Vidyadhar Chakravarti, chief architect from Bengal who with Jai Singh's approval founded a city on strong scientific principles, built in less than eight years. Laid out according to the Shilpa Shastra an ancient Hindu treatise on architecture, it still remains one of India's best planned cities. The city has been divided into nine blocks of which two are kept for the City Palace Complex, the Jantar Mantar, the Janana Mahals and other state buildings, whereas the other seven

*Birla Temple*

have been made to the existing complex by successive rulers. Some of the maharajas filled the palace with scientific and artistic treasures, while others focused on public works. The palace is now a museum.

The complex built in a delightful mix of Rajput and Mughal styles of architecture, can be entered through the Sirekh-ki-Deorhi gate on the eastern side leading to the outer court or Jaleb Chowk which also houses several other buildings like the Nakkar Khana or the drum house. In the center of the courtyard lies the Mubarak Mahal, a two-storeyed marble building built by Madho Singh II in 1900. This beautiful palace has exquisitely-carved screens and scalloped arches on its exterior walls to give it a delicate appearance. Earlier, functioning as a state secretariat and then as a guest house, today it is a textile museum displaying an exciting range of dresses worn by the royalty. The Sileh Khana in the north-west corner of the courtyard contains an awesome collection of traditional armoury which is among the finest in the country.

blocks were earmarked for the public. The city was encircled by the city wall, which opened at seven gates or darwazas. The city wasn't just aesthetically beautiful, but also virtually impregnable. The sense of security it gave the citizens encouraged trading, arts and culture flourished and the city prospered.

The **City Palace or Chandra Mahal** is in the center of Jaipur and covers 1/7th or 15 per cent of the Pink City's area. It was built between 1729 and 1732 by Jai Singh. The palace is surrounded by a high wall within which are a series of courtyards, gardens and other buildings. Additions

Two extraordinary marble elephants carved out of a single piece of marble standing at the gleaming entrance of Rajendra Pol are significant because they were gifted at the birth of erstwhile Maharaja Bhawani Singh. There was tremendous jubilation because a male heir was born in the royal family after nearly a century. Beyond the gateway is the pillared courtyard of Diwan-I-Khas which was used during special occasions. Built on an open-arched plan, it houses two massive silver urns, each weighing more than 2,000 kilos and having a capacity to hold 1,800 gallons of water each. These were used to carry the holy Ganga Jal when Madho Singh II went to Britain in 1900, the first Kachchwaha ruler to do so. The famous Ridhi Sidhi Pol has a courtyard with four beautifully-decorated gates depicting the moods of the peacock in exquisite frescoes. Close to it, lies the luxurious and opulent Chandra Mahal built by Jai Singh II with further additions made by successive rulers. The creamy-white ornamental palace has seven storeys, each floor having been decorated differently. One section of the magnificent palace is still the royal residence of the ex-Maharaja. On the other side of the palace complex lies the Diwan-I-Am now converted into a museum exhibiting a rare collection of ancient manuscripts, portraits, palanquins, chandeliers, a golden throne and a fascinating range of priceless miniature paintings in the Rajput style. To the north of Chandra Mahal lies the famous 18th century temple of Govind Devji, which enshrines the idol of Lord Krishna, the family deity of the Jaipur royalty. The palace opened to tourists in 1950s and to motion pictures. 400 films have been shot here including North by Northwest and Errol Flynn's Kim.

East of the Chandra Mahal is the **Jantar Mantar**. It is an open air observatory which was designed by Maharaja Jai Singh in 1728. Before commencing the observatory, he sent scholars abroad to study other foreign observatories so that he would have one that would satisfy his passion for astronomy. In order to achieve accuracy, the instruments were made from stone and marble. Each of these curious sculptures has a specific purpose such as measuring the positions of stars, altitudes, and azimuths and calculating the times of eclipses. The most striking instrument is the sundial with its 27m-high gnomon (the rod of the sundial).

**Jaigarh Fort** was built in 1726 by Jai Singh. Jaigarh, completed in the 18th Century, is perched majestically atop a

*Temple complex at Galta*

79

*Interior view of City Palace with Chandra Mahal in the background*

ragged hill which enables the viewer a spectacular view of the Amber valley. The armoury in the fort has a large collection of swords and small arms. There is a cannon foundry where the barrels were cast and one can still see the pits. There is also an enormous 50 tonne cannon known as the Jayvana, which stands on top of a tower and is supposed to be the largest cannon on wheels in the world. The barrel measures 8m in diameter and has a range of around 35 kms, but has never been used. The fort was the treasury of the Kuchhwahas and people still believe that some part of the fort still holds gold bullion. During the Emergency in 1976, the government ransacked the fort, emptied the reservoirs of water (where the gold was supposed to have been buried), but found nothing. The central courtyard has three enormous underground water tanks, one used by prisoners for bathing, one that was said to hold the gold and jewels and one which was empty. There are also gardens, a granary, the 10th century temple of Ram harihar and the 12th century temple of Kal Bhairav. There are dark passageways among the palaces and one can see a collection of coins and puppets. It is a remarkable feat of military architecture and is pretty well preserved, mainly because the fort was never captured.

*A painting in the interiors of City Palace*
**Page no. 82-83** : *Jantar Mantar, an open air observatory*

Another of Sawai Jai Singh's creations which was later extended by Sawai Ram Singh, **Nahargarh or the Tiger Fort**, stands atop a sheer ridge. It was built in 1734 by Jai Singh as a retreat for his wives. Further additions were made in 1868.

The fort itself is in ruins, but some of the original painted floral patterns on the walls remain, and some of the rooms furnished for the maharajas. All the queen's apartments are identical, arranged around the central courtyard in perfect symmetry, each with a room for a personal maidservant. The design of the apartments are regular and repetitive in contrast to the other royal dwellings in Jaipur.

*Overview of Chandra Mahal from the entrance*

*Overview of Chandra Mahal*

*Mubarak Mahal*

*Peacock Gate inside City Palace*

Jai Singh's II death in 1743, led to a battle of succession and internal strife. Many maharajas ruled Jaipur but later Maharaja. **Sawai Pratap Singh** ruled from 1778 to 1803. He is known as the great ruler of Jaipur for his devotion to Lord Krishna. The fountains behind the Govind Dev temple are credited to him. Writing under the penname Brijnidhi, he composed many poems and songs in large variety of meters.

The finest example of his connoisseur ship is the unique monuments of **Hawa Mahal** - the place of the Winds. The Hawa Mahal, part of the City Palace complex, is a familiar landmark, and looks like a series of pierced windows placed in tiers to overlook the street below. This odd pyramidical-shaped, five-storeyed structure was built by Maharaja Pratap Singh in 1799. The top three floors of this uniquely-designed building are just a room deep while the lower sections have connected rooms and courtyards. The tapering faôade with 953 latticed windows, perforated screens and projecting balconies lend a delicate fringe to this airy structure which is actually the rear portion of the building. Its purpose was simply to allow the royal women a view of ceremonial processions while seated behind the small windows, allowing them to look out without themselves being seen.

**Sawai Ram Singh II** reigned from 1835 till 1880. He was known as the colourful Maharaja. During his rule Jaipur was named **Pink City**, the reason for the autumnal colours on the facades of all old city buildings was a forthcoming trip by the Prince of Wales (later King Edward VII) in 1876 for whom the capital was being decorated. The colour was chosen after several experiments to cut down the intense glare from the reflection of the blazing rays of the sun. To this day, the buildings are uniformly rose pink.

In the 1868 A.D. **Sawai Ram Singh II** built **Ram Niwas Bagh**, a lush spacious garden with a zoo, an aviary, a greenhouse, a herbarlum, a museum and popular sport ground as a famine relief project. The Albert Hall Museum-fine example of Indo Sarcenic style of architecture designed by Sir Swinton Jacob, was opened later with an exquisite collection of sculptures, paintings, decorative wares, natural history specimen, and Egyptian mummy and the celebrated Persian carpet.

**Madho Singh II** (1880-1922) was the next ruler after Ram Singh II. His clothes and other items can be seen at the Maharaja Sawai Man Singh II museum. One remarkable exhibit in set of voluminous clothes of Madho Singh II who was over two meters tall, 1.3m wide and weighed 225 kg. He had made a lot of progress to the State of Jaipur.

**Sawai Man Singh II** reigned from 1922 till 1949 when India had already gained Independence in 1947. He became Rajpramukh or the head of the newly formed Rajasthan union. He improved the water supply by building Ram Garh that supplied water to Jaipur. During his reign, civic buildings such as schools, hospitals and secretariats were built outside the original walls.

The people of Jaipur like any other part of Rajasthan are known for their colourful attires. The streets and market places of Jaipur still witnesses scenes of turbaned Rajasthani men, moving around with their women, who are dressed in swirling skirts called lehengas and odhni or veil with flashing Meenakari (enamel) jewellery that bring to life all the colours of the desert.

These colourful fabrics are either printed in dyes or embroidered and seldom worn plain. Sanganer and Bagru, the two towns on the outskirts of Jaipur, specialize in traditional block-printing textiles,

*A view from the arch (City Palace)*

*The largest silver pot used to store Holy Ganga Water*

*Interior view of City Palace*

*A musician playing the Instrument inside City Palace*

85

*Ram Yantra*

wherein wooden blocks carved with floral and geometric patterns and symbolic motifs are dipped in vegetable colours made from extracts of flowers and minerals, and then hand printed and dried.

*The Unnatansha Yantra*

Jaipur is also famous for semi-precious stones and the best place to buy is from Johari Bazaar. Miniature, handicrafts, clothes, jewellery of silver and lac are other items to be bought in Jaipur. A rakhri for the forehead, nath for the nose, paijeb for the ankles along with a necklace, waistband and a large set of

lac bangles worn almost all over the arm are among favourite possessions of Rajasthani womens. Leather or camel hide mojris (footwear) embroidered with thread, appliquÈ or beadwork are known for their comfort and elegance. The handmade paper from Sanganer is also much in demand all over the world.

While the terracotta is among the hed

*Yantra Raj*

earliest craft traditions of Rajputana, the concept of blue pottery is confined only to Jaipur. This Persian art does not involve the use of clay but Fuller's earth mixed with sodium sulphate and crushed quartz to mould different items decorated with motifs in different shades of blue and green.

*Chakra Yantra*

86

*Jai Prakash Yantra*

*Maharaja Sawai Jai Singh II*

*Sun Dial*

*Kranti Writta Yantra*

*Narivalaya Yantra*

*Chakra Yantra*

*The Sun Dial Small*

*Yantra Raj*

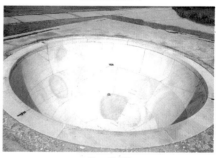

*Kapali 'B'*

*Ram Yantra*

*Digansha Yantra*

*Chakra Yantra*

# AMER

*Amer Fort*

The cultural prosperity of Rajasthan is evident in its local festivals some of which attract international attention. The most important being the Elephant Festival gets underway in the month of Phalgun (March) on the eve of Holi, the festival of colours. It is famous for its procession of elephants, camels, horses and folk dancers. The sight of mighty jumbos striding majestically is a treat to watch. Events at the festival include, a polo match, the Elephant race, the tug-of-war between an elephant and nineteen men. Gangaur festival is a unique festival held annually in honour of goddess Gauri, few days after Holi. Primarily a festival for women, married women pray for their husbands and unmarried girls pray for getting a good husband. Festive processions are taken out, women draw water from wells, pick flowers, and chant hymns to the goddess Parvati. Teej is a major event in Jaipur. The festival is celebrated during the months of July/August and dedicated to goddess parvati. The festival celebrates the beginning of the monsoon. The Chaksu Fair is held on Shitla Ashtami in March every year and prayers and special food items are

*Amer Fort*

*Ganesh Pole*
***Page no. 89 : Top (L) :*** *Tope inside Jai Garh Fort* ***(R)*** *: Screen inside Amer Fort*
***Centre (L) :*** *Jagat Sarvan Temple* ***(R)*** *: Decorated elephants*
***Bottom (L) :*** *Elephant stand at Amer Fort* ***(R) :*** *Sheesh Mahal*
*Below : Baradari near Diwan-I-Aam, Amer Palace*

*Shila Devi Temple inside Amer Fort*
**Page no. 91 : Top (L) :** *Ganesh Pole with Diwan-I-Aam* **(R) :** *Amer Fort*
**Centre (L) :** *A decorated elephant* **(R) :** *Jal Mahal*
**Bottom :** *An Elephant festival*
**Below :** *An elephant performing during the festival*

offered to Goddess Shitla to protect the people from smallpox. Naag panchami celebrated in July/August is dedicated to snake deities who are said to have associations with Hindu gods and goddesses. These festivals bring the people closer to one another.

Jaipur firmly holds its position on the world tourist map. A status, which has been bestowed on it due to its vibrant lifestyle, colourful people and a history that is full of stories, reflecting the bravery of those who occupied this region in the past.

**Page no. 92 :** *Top (L) :* *A decorated camel*
*(R) :* *Ladies dressed traditionally for Gangaur Festival*
*Centre (L) :* *A famous dancer during her performance*
*(R) :* *Rajasthani Folk Dance*
*Bottom (L) :* *Ladies bathing along the riverside*
*(R) :* *A traditional Rahjasthani woman*

*Dargah Ajmer Sharrif*

*Traditional Rajasthani Jewellery*

*A view of Pushkar Ghat*

**Page no. 94 :**
*Different moods of Rajasthan*

**Page no. 95 :**
*Top (L , R and Bottom L,) :*
*Traditional Rajasthani Ladies*

**Bottom (R) :** *Famous cloth painting of Rajasthan*